HOW TO BE
SUCCESSFUL IN WHAT
YOU WANT TO BE

Other books by the author

(1) *The Price For The Buffalo* (fiction)

(2) *A Harvest From Betrayals* (fiction)

(3) *Secrets Of Passing Mathematics Without Difficulties* (Non fiction)

(4) Political irony and other poems

HOW TO BE SUCCESSFUL IN WHAT YOU WANT TO BE

AKIMUA TIMITIMI

To order additional copies of this book, contact:
Xlibris
1-888-795-4274
www.Xlibris.com
Orders@Xlibris.com
551723

TABLE OF CONTENTS

To God the source of all wisdom

WITHIN US

Within us lie trees of wines,
Seeing in us such might,
let us tap the vines,
To dine in dimes.

Within us hides a name,
feeling in us such fames
let us search the books,
to find a page it glues

Within us lies a mine
even though rigs we have not
let us dig with what we have got,
to wear our robes in gold,

Within us lies a sea,
living in us such feats
let us fish in such things
to reap in all the gifts.

Akimua Timitmi
(An extract from my Anthology "Political Irony and other Poems")

PREFACE

I have been able to come up with this book because of the importance I have seen before encouragement in life. Often times what that people need to move to the next step in life or to come out of affliction. I also use this principle to overcome many situations. Money is not all that a man needs. As the body needs food so does the soul need food. I do hope this book will touch and lift all those who come across it.

Akimua Timitmi

"We give rudiments of reverence to the body but regard as nothing the rape of the human mind."

INTRODUCTION

Words have power to lift you to the next steps. I was watching a film "**The Arabian Nights**" where a woman was encouraging her discouraged husband, a king who was to be attacked by another king. The method she employed was the theme of the film the "Arabian Nights'. It was a series of stories she told her husband in the night. Stories about great deeds, how people used their wits and courage to conquer, escaped great dangers and subdued kingdoms. Each time the king started his fits of fears she told him a story. Finally the king summoned courage gingered by those stories went up and took the bull by the horn and won his battle. That is what the bible primarily is, stories to push you on. All scriptures is given for information (2nd timothy 3: 11-17) so that we can learn from the faith of others.

Words can demoralize and can also mobilize a man. The Bible likened the word of God as a two edged sword, which can reach the soul to bring it up or down depending on how it is used. Most of the words used here are not exact quotation from the bible some are my own words, but the truth is always the truth. Gold will always be gold where-ever it is found, in the dustbin or in the alter.

HOW TO USE THIS BOOK

You can start reading from any topic that affects your situation or start from the beginning and read through to the end. After enough assimilation, it is your moral duty to pass the information to others in similar situations. Note that knowledge can be likened to a volatile liquid that vaporizes easily, so you need to keep a copy for yourself in order to revisit it when ever the need arises. You can also help your friends by buying copies for them *"Wisdom is better than silver and gold."*

"Give a man fish and you feed him for a day but teach a man how to fish and you feed him for life."

A Chinese proverb

ABOUT WORDS

"Without knowing the force of words it in impossible to know men."

Confucius

(1) The safest words are always those which bring us most directly to facts.
(2) Eating words does not give indigestion.
(3) The soul like the body live on what it feeds on.
(4) Pithy sentences are like sharp nails which force truth upon our memory.
(5) All maxims have their antagonist maxims, proverbs should be sold in pairs, a single one being but a half truth.

Pleasant words are like honey comb sweatiness to the soul and health to the bones (proverbs 16: 24)

PART A

DESTINY

(1) Whatsoever a man sowed so shall he reap.

In the Old Testament, from reading the history of the Israelites we can deduce that God pronounced his anger according to the actions of the Israelites but did the things his covenant stated. In his anger he said, "He will visit the iniquity of the father upon their children's children. But in the book of Ezekiel he said that "the wickedness of a father will be upon the father ... and the righteousness of the son will be upon the son" Ezekiel" 18: 4 - 14 - 17 the Ezekiel covenant in more current than that of Genesis so why be old fashioned "Because he remembered that man was a mortal being" Genesis 8: 21

God changed his decision to use the levites <u>instead</u> of the first born children from Israel. Number 3:12

Reject any negative deeds that your parents, tribe, race did as your destiny. You are a separate entity a unique being. You have your own cross to carry and it's rewards not your parents or tribe's curses'. Believe and act that the set backs that you did not sow of your tribe and race will not be the set backs you will reap.

Isaiah 1:18 "come now let us reason together saith the lord though your sins be as scarlet they shall be as white as snow"

His anger is but for a moment his right hand are pleasures forever more. Change from the setbacks to the checkbooks. When Cain was banished he cried unto God that his burden was too much for him and God lightened his burden.

Genesis 4:13 –15

Ask God to remove those burdens from you.

(2) DESTINY is not matter of chance. It is a matter of choice. It is not a thing to be waited for it is a thing to achieved.
(3) Lots of people confuse bad management with destiny.
(4) Destiny is a tyrant's authority for crime and a fools excuse for failure.
(5) Men heap together the mistakes of their lives, and create a monster they call destiny.
(6) In God's business it is allowed to come from anywhere but it is not allowed to stay anywhere than at the top Genesis 28:13.

"He will not withhold any good thing from you"
"His thoughts towards you are thought of goodwill"

LADDERS TO YOUR DESTINY

THOUGHTS

(1) Thought is an idea or pattern of ideas.
(2) As a man thinketh so he is.
(3) Great thoughts reduced to practice become great acts.
(4) You are today where your thought have brought you: you will be tomorrow where your thought will take you.
(5) The soul of God is poured into the world through the thoughts of men.
(6) The spirit of man is the candle of the lord.
(7) Learning without thought is labour lost.

VISION

(1) You see things and you say "why?" but vision is I dream things that never were and I say "why not?"
(2) Dreaming is an act of pure imagination, attesting in all men a creative power, which, if it were available in waking would make every man a Dante or Shakespeare.

(3) Where there is no vision the people perish.

(4) It is never safe to look into the future with the eyes of fear.

(5) No man that does not see vision will ever realize any high hope or undertake any high enterprise.

(6) If one advances confidently in the direction of his dreams and endeavors to live the life, which he has imagined, he will meet with a success unexpected in common hours.

(7) All men of action are dreamers.

(8) The end of wisdom is to dream high enough to lose the dream in the seeking of it.

(9) It is difficult to say what is impossible, for the dream of yesterday is the hope of today and the reality of tomorrow

PURPOSE, AIMS, AMBITION

(1) Great minds have purpose, others have wishes.

(2) Only the consciousness of a purpose that is mightier than any man and worthy of all men can fortify and inspirit and compose the souls of men.

(3) The good man is the man who no matter how morally unworthy he has been, is moving to become better.

(4) Aim at the sun and you may not reach it. But your arrow will fly far higher than if aimed at an object on a level with yourself.

(5) In great attempts it is glorious even to fall.

(6) Not failure but low aim is crime.

(7) High aims form high characters and great objects bring out great minds.

(8) Ambition is the last refuge of failure.

(9) Too low they build who build below the sky.

(10) Drive your car to a star.

(11) He who surpasses or subdues mankind must look down on the hate of those below.

(12) All ambitions are lawful except those which climb upward on the miseries or credulities of mankind.

(13) The men who succeed are the efficient few, they are the few who have will power and will power to develop themselves.

(14) No bird soars too high if he soars with his own wings.

(15) It seems we can never give up longing and wishing while we are thoroughly alive. There are certain things we feel to be beautiful and good and we must hunger after them.

(16) The very substance of the ambitious is merely the shadow of a dream.

(17) Finally whatsoever things are true whatsoever things are noble whatsoever things are just whatsoever things are pure whatsoever things are lovely whatsoever things are of good report, if there is any thing praise worthy meditate on these things Philippians 4:8

EVALUATION, FORESIGHT

One of the problems of carrier dissatisfaction is the inability of people to have foresight or evaluate whatever action they would take. <u>That is the end result.</u> This factor is responsible for a person doing first a course and changing to another course after graduating supposedly after reaching a brick wall. It is equally responsible for broken marriages.

(1) Evaluation is seeing your self as the person you want to be example, the architect, doctor, musician etc.

A lot of people want to be something, do something but without knowing the implications, Esther in the bible knew the consequences of her action if she saw the king, success or death.

I have heard of female medical students who fainted on first seeing a cadaver (corpse) they thought medicine was just the ability to read. You must know that you will see blood, experience deaths, and have the ability to read for hours, know the Job prospects.

The engineer: in evaluating example the electrical or mechanical engineer, he must know that he needs knowledge of mathematics, the types of job he will be involved in, sometimes very dirty, sometimes in distance rural areas far from his home and loved ones facing hazards.

The musician: in evaluating your ambition as a musician you will asses your self on the income you will make if successful. The sleepless nights you will have in entertaining late into the night and the odd places you will go on invitations.

IN MARRIAGE OR RUNNING A FAMILY. How is your intended wife/ husband? Do you want to live with a talkative, a fighter, a man who travels a lot or a nurse? That is evaluation. One has to think of training his kids, pay hospital bills, school fees and clothes his family. It involves money! Love is not money.

An example of an evaluation or foresight done by an advertising agent of a fishing company in Alaska U S A went as follows:

VACANCY

Fishing company jobs in Alaska.

(1) Can you withstand intensive cold.
(2) Work in high sea?
(3) Withstand sea sickness or be thrown to sharks if you plan to runaway halfway into the job, if yes.

Then apply to the manager... you already know what is involved so it is up to you to apply or not.

Is The Goal Achievable?

"Which of you when building a home will not first count the cost" luke14:28-30

Jesus Christ

Action to be effective must be directed to clearly conceived ends.

PLANNING

(1) After seeing your-self as the person you want to be, the next step is planning, not the other way round.
(2) Planning is to devise a program of action for vision.
(3) Toil, feel, think hope, you will be sure to dream enough before you die, without planning.

(4) War fare is neither won by just the arsenal an army has nor by the number of soldiers of valor or strength but also by the gray heads of the planning generals.

(5) A building that is well planned is orderly finished without having to chisel off unnecessary protrusions.

(6) Take a cue from the bees for with planning the drones scout for nectar the workers feed the lava and the queen lays the eggs.

(7) Planning is the foundation for specialization for we can now all have a role to play well in life.

(8) Chance favors the prepared mind.

DECISION, WILL, COURAGE

(1) Decision is the result of making up one's mind

(2) When possible make the decisions now, even if acting is in the future. A reviewed decision usually is better than one reached at the last moment.

(3) It does not take much strength to do things but it requires great strength to decide on what to do.

(4) It is not good to do things by halves if it be rights do it bodily if it be wrong leave it undone.

(5) You cannot run away from weakness, you must some time fight it out or perish, and if that be so, why not now and where you stand.

(6) A journey of a thousand mile starts with a step.

(7) There is no more miserable human being than one in whom nothing is habitual but indecision.

(8) While the mind is in doubt it is driven this way and that way by a slight impulse.

(9) He is no wise man who will quit certainty for uncertainty.

(10) Indecision is debilitating; it feeds upon itself. It is, one might almost say, habit forming not only that but it is contagious, it transmits itself to others.

(11) Indecision has often given an advantage to the other fellow because he did his thinking beforehand.

(12) People do not lack strength they lack will.

(13) Great souls have wills; feeble ones have wishes.

(14) Will is character in action.

(15) Strength does not come from physical capacity. it comes from an indomitable will.

(16) No action will be considered, blameless unless the will was so for by the will the act was dictated.

(17) Courage is almost a contradiction in terms; it means a strong desire to live taking the form of readiness to die.

(18) It takes vision and courage to create it takes faith and courage to prove.

(19) Courage is resistance to fear mastery of fear-not absence of fear.

(20) This is no time for ease and comfort it is time to dare and endure.

(21) For better it is to dare mighty things, to win glorious triumphs, even thought checkered by failure, than to take rank with those poor spirits who neither enjoy much nor suffer much, because they live in the gray twilight that knows not victory nor fear.

(22) Last but by no means least, courage-moral courage the courage of one's convictions, the courage to see things through. The world is in a constant conspiracy against the brave. It's the age-old struggle –the roar of the crowd on one side and the voice of your conscience on the other.

(23) A prayer:-give us the fortitude to endure the things which cannot be changed the things which should be changed, courage to change the things which can be changed and the wisdom to know one from the other.

(24) Courage is like a ball seeing the net and not the defenders

RISK TAKING

(1)   The policy of being too cautions is the greater risk of all.

(2)   The willingness to take risks is our grasp of faith.

(3)   Don't be afraid to take a big step if one is indicated you can't cross a ditch in two small jumps.

(4)   Every noble acquisition is attended with its risks, he who fears to encounter, that person must not expect to obtain the other.

(5)   Who bravely dares must sometimes risk a fall.

(6)   A ship in a harbor is safe but that is not what ships are built for.

(7)   Fortune is the rod of the weak and the staff of the brave.

HOW TO HAVE WILL

EXERCISE: Before any endeavor you think you cannot do and decision, then recite this to yourself.

(1) "I can, I can, I can I can, I can," till it is in your subconscious.
(2) Pray for boldness; recite, "I can do all things through Christ who straightens me."

Choose the one you feel according to your beliefs.

OPPORTUNISM

Opportunism: is the practice of adjusting one's policy in the light of each new situation, as it arises not according to principle or plan. Opportunity is a set of circumstances providing a chance or possibilities. To seize opportunity to one's advantage, one has to be an opportunist.

(1) The bible has always been there but only the opportunists tap from its wealth of knowledge.
(2) An opportunist uses the sand by his seashore to build the mansion in his visions and the woods by his room to build his roof.
(3) A wise man will make more opportunities than he will find.
(4) You will never find time for any thing. If you want time you must make it.
(5) Do not wait for extra ordinary circumstances to do good; try use ordinary situations.
(6) The commonest form, one of the most often neglected and the safest opportunity for the average man to seize is hard work.

Joseph's ascension to the second in command to pharaoh was his ability to use an opportunity in prison. After interpreting the dream of the steward he saw an opportunity and reminded him to remember him when he would be serving the king again Genesis 40:14. King David of the bible-fame used the opportunity of Goliath to display his skills in the use of his sling to gain the favors of admirers and later followers as an adept leader. Samson's final defeat of the philistines was not only the use of his strength but also the use of an opportunity. Chickens don't wait for food to feed but use the opportunity of where they are to search for what they can.

(7) Shallow men believe in lack, strong men believe in cause and effect.
(8) Chance favors the prepared mind.
(9) Good luck is a lazy man's estimate of a workers success.
(10) A pound of pluck is worth a ton of luck.
(11) If a man be lucky there is no foretelling the extent of his fortune. Push him into an ocean and like it or not, he will swim out with a pearl in his hand, put him in a desert he will make a glass out of sand and discover an oak.

ACTION

(1) This is the process of doing something.
(2) Actions speak louder than words.
(3) Actions may not always bring happiness but there is no happiness without actions.
(4) It is by acts and not by ideas that people live.
(5) Thoughts and theory precede all salutary action, yet action is nobler in itself than either thoughts or theory.
(6) You can't cross the sea merely by standing and staring at the water. Don't let yourself indulge in vain wishes.
(7) I don't like these cold precise perfect people, who in order to do wrong never do wrong never do anything.
(8) To avoid critism do nothing say nothing be nothing.
(9) Do not attempt to do a thing unless you are sure of yourself but do not relinquish it simply because someone else is not one of you.
(10) Thought is the blossom, language the bud, action the fruit behind it.
(11) Position anything is better than negative nothing.
(12) The actions of men are the best interpretations of their thoughts
(13) Think like a man of action, act like a man of thought.
(14) What you do speaks so loud that I cannot hear what you say.
(15) Action may not always bring happiness but there is no happiness without action.
(16) The chief danger in life is that you take too many precautions.

(17) The cowards never started and the weak died along the way.

(18) Great occasions do not make heroes or cowards they simply unveil them to the eyes of men.

(19) To know what is right and not do it is the worst cowardice.

(20) The people to fear are not those who disagree with you but those who disagree with you and are too cowardly and lack action to let you know.

(21) Faint hearts never won a fair lady.

(22) How many feasible project have miscarried through despondency and been strangled in their birth by a coward imagination.

(23) A cowardly call barks more fiercely them it bikes.

(24) At the bottom of a good deal of the bravery that appears in the world there larks a miserable cowardice. Men will face bullets and steel because they cannot act to face public opinions.

(25) Even if you are on the right track-you will get run over if you just sit there.

(26) Never that till tomorrow, which you can do today.

(27) Putting off an easy thing makes it hard and putting off a hard one makes it impossible.

(28) Shallow men believe in luck strong men believe in course and effect.

DILIGENCE

(1) The expectations of life depend upon diligence; the mechanic that would perform his work must first sharpen his tools.

(2) Diligence is the mother of good luck.

(3) He who labors diligently need never despair for all things are accomplish by diligence and labor.

(4) What we hope ever to do with ease, we must first learn to do with diligence.

(5) Few things are impossibly to diligence and skill... Great works are performed, not by strength but by perseverance.

(6) No thoroughly occupied man was ever yet very miserable.

(7) It is better to wear out than to rust out.

(8) The more we do the more we can do.

(9) "Give a man fish you feed him for a day but teach a man how to fish and you feed him for life." A Chinese proverb.

(10) A man who gives his children habits of industry provides for them better than by giving them a fortune.

(11) If you have great talents, industry will improve them. If moderate abilities, industry will supply their deficiencies nothing is denied to well directed labor nothing is ever to be attained without it.

(12) In the ordinary business of life, industry can do anything which genius can do, and very many things, which it cannot.

(13) Genius is one percent inspiration ninety percent hard work.

(14) The fruit derived from labour is the sweetest fruit of all.

(15) Excellence in any department can be attained only by the labour of a lifetime, it is not to be purchased at a lesser price.

(16) It is only through labour and painful effort by grim energy and resolute courage that we move on to better things.

(17) Pity the man who wants a coat so cheap that the man or woman who produces the cloth will starve in the process.

(18) The old commandment God gave to man was six days work and keep the seventh day hallowed, God himself lived by an example. A man is a worker. If he is not he is nothing.

(19) Work should be taken as part of living and not suffering, then it will be enjoyed.

(20) Work is the greatest thing in the world so we should always save some for tomorrow.

(21) Things don't turn up in this word unless somebody turns them up.

(22) Fortune is ever seen accompanying industry.

(23) Fortune is a great deceiver she sells herself very dear the things she seems to give us.

(24) Good luck is a lazy man's estimate of a worker's success.

(25) A pound of pluck is worth a ton of luck.

A SPIRIT OF COMPETITION

Competition and perfection are closely related. Competition brings out the best in a man. Without competition, there would be no champions. It is a common phenomenon in the soft drink world, Coca-Cola versus Pepsi products. Competition makes one company strive to outdo the other in terms of advertisement, promotion and production of better goods. If there are no competitions, there will be no standards or records set.

When Israel was captured by Gideon to fight with the Midianites, God did a selection by indirect competition. For him to select the best of the soldiers, he eliminated those who were fearful and afraid and were not alert/people who did not (lap water) Judges 7:1-7 – King James Version

(1) "Then Jerobbaal, who is Gideon, and all the people that were with him, rose up early and pitched beside the well of Harod; so that the host of Midianites were on the north side of them, by the hill of Moreh, the valley.

(2) And the lord said unto Gideon "the people that are with thee are too many for me to give the Midianites into their hands, lest Israel vaunt themselves against me, saying mine own arm hath saved me.

(3) Now therefore go to proclaim in the ears of the people saying, whosoever is fearful and afraid, let him return and depart easily from mount Gilead. And there returned of the people twenty and two thousand and there remained ten thousand.

(4) And the Lord said unto Gideon, the people are yet too many; bring them down into the water, and I will try them for thee there; and it shall be that of whom I say unto thee. This shall go with thee, the same shall go with thee and of whomsoever I say unto thee, this shall not go with thee, the same shall not go.

(5) So he brought down the people unto the water; and the Lord said unto Gideon, every one that lappeth, as a dog lappeth, him shall thou set by himself; likewise everyone that boweth down upon his knees to drink.

(6) And the number of them that lapped, putting their hand to their mouth, were three hundred men; but all the rest of the people bowed down upon their knees to drink water.

(7) And the Lord said unto Gideon, by the three hundred men that lapped will I save you, and deliver the Midianites into thy hand; and let all the other people go every man unto his place".

PERSEVERANCE, PATIENCE

(1) This is the ability to try hard in spite of obstacles and difficulties. The quality of being persistent and persevering.

(2) Perseverance is continuing in a state of grace leading to a state of glory.

(3) Persistence is not falling although withered.

(4) The difference between perseverance and obstinacy is, that one often comes from a strong will, and the other from a strong wont.

(5) Persistence is like the postage stamp, which succeeds through its ability to stick to one thing till it gets there.

(6) We make way for the man who boldly pushes past us.

(7) There is no failure except in no longer trying. There is no defeat except from within no really insurmountable barrier save our own inherent weakness of purpose.

(8) Perseverance is more prevailing than violence and many things which cannot be overcome when they are together yield themselves up when taken little by little.

(9) Little continuous drops of water can cause a mighty ocean.

(10) Endurance is patience concentrated.

(11) Concentration is the secret of strength.

(12) Adopt the pace of nature, her secret is patience and perseverance.

(13) He that can have perseverance can have what he will.

(14) Patience is bitter but its fruit is sweet.

(15) Under the sun there is a time for every thing.

(16) Patience and time do more than strength or passions.

(17) The secret of success is constancy of purpose.

(18) There is no such thing as an inevitable war. If war comes it will be from failure of human wisdom to persist in dialogue.

(19) Not in rewards but in the strength to strive, the blessing lies.

(20) The rewards of a thing well done is to have done it.

In my introduction I mentioned a story concerning the Arabian nights. One of the stories was about a king that was almost defeated and in despair he was in the forest and observed something, as he was about to sleep off. He saw a spider making its web. Almost at the edge of completion, a bird that was looking for larva on the tree where the spider was dived at a larva and destroyed the spider's web. The spider started all over again. Another bird saw larva and dived for it destroying its web again. This went on an on till all the larva had been picked up by the ravens birds each time destroying the spider's web. Nonetheless the spider was consistent each time rebuilding its web whenever it was destroyed because that was its trap for insects for its survival. When the almost defeated king saw this unparallel act of perseverance in the spider, he summoned courage and picked his remaining soldiers always visualizing the persistent spider and attacked his adversaries who were now having a half-victory celebration. He won his battle.

FAITH, PROVIDENCE, PRAYER (SUPERNATURAL)

Faith simply means trust, confidence. In religion it is the complete acceptance of a truth which cannot be demonstrated or proved by the process of logical thoughts. In Christianity it is the virtue with which a Christian believes in the revealed truths of God. Faith can be divided into three major types.

(1)   Faith in ones' self (2) Faith in what you are doing and (3) faith in the supernatural or what I can refer to as providence.

(1)   *Faith in oneself and others working with you, to achieve your destiny*. Another way of describing such a faith is <u>self-confidence.</u> A man must have dogged self-confidence in his abilities so as to be able to surmount any critisms in pursuit of his goals. Paul of the bible expressed this in the words "I can do all things through Christ who strengthens me." Self-confidence made David of the bible-fame stand against the giant Goliath of the philistines. Most of the scientific discoveries were done because the people believed in themselves and others working with them. The founder of Ford motors believed he could make a

car with double engine that had never been done. There where critisms along the way but self-confidence in others who knew it better than him pushed him on till he succeeded. Bill Gates of the Microsoft computer equally used this principle to add icons to computers, which made Microsoft products unique. Although he did not discover computers he believed he could improve on it. Self-confidence can be gotten by emulating others who have similar abilities. He that walks with wise men becomes wise. Self-confidence can also be increased by previous deeds. David believed he could defeat Goliath because he had defeated fiercer foes- a lion and a bear so who was Goliath? Public opinion is a weak tyrant compared with our private opinion. what a man thinks of himself that is which determines or rather indicate his fate. See yourself as very handsome or beautiful, a replica of God. say it to yourself.

(2) The only limit to our realization of tomorrow will be our doubts of today.
(3) The optimist proclaims that we live in the best of all possible worlds; and the pessimist fears this is true.
(4) The habit of looking on the bright side of every event is worth more, than a thousand pounds a year.

However what I will add is that the blessings of God added no sorrow the steps of a righteous man are by the lord. Psalm 37:23

(2) *Faith in the supernatural (prayer, providence).* The essence of all religions today is the belief in celestial or supernatural beings that can help them when they cannot help themselves again. There was an inscription I read somewhere which said "God will only come in when we do not have anything else to do." David of the bible always took advantage of the supernatural. David never did anything until he enquired from God. His belief in God made him say the popular psalm 23 "The lord is my shepard..." The use of the supernatural can be positive or negative. Elisha used it for the negative by telling a bear to consume kids that called him a bald head 2 king 2:23-24. I will not go more than I know in this area but the supernatural

exists. Norman Vincent Pearle the author of "The Power of Positive Thinking." also acknowledged this fact in that book. However what I will add is that the blessings of God added no sorrows. The lord orders the steps of a righteous man. Psalm37:23

(5) ... but the people who know their God shall be strong and do exploits. Daniel11:23

AN ARITHMETIC OF FAITH

(1) *Favors (providence) plus hard work equals success.*
   Hard work minus Favors (providence) equals struggling.
   Faith (providence) minus works equals dead faith.

Faith and use of the supernatural is achieved when one is well informed about the practices involved in a particular religion. This could be read in Acts of the apostles' story of Paul and the seven sons of Sceva. Acts 19:11. Paul could perform in the supernatural because he know the source of his power and how to invite it to achieve his aim while the sons Sceva could be termed as religious fanatics who believed in something but in an improper way and could not utilize it. Such is a case of half-knowledge. Knowledge of the supernatural involves proper information. Paul once said his books should be brought to him for consultation. The younger prophets in the Old Testament were always seen in company of the older ones understudying them for knowledge. No man is an embedment of knowledge that is why every one has to learn what he does not know. The knowledge of the supernatural involves the knowledge of the rules and virtues (some of which I have used as "ladders to destiny." here) the supernatural can aid man in addition with other humans too and human relation has to be taught to people for proper utilization.

(2) Supernatural intention is as a result of knowing all the rules, virtues of the supernatural for effective result.

Elisha used the supernatural knowledge (miracle) to make an axe float on water.

2 kings 6:5-6

Key to the supernatural. Ask questions why?, How?, then research. This is the key to all discoveries!

"The longer I live, the more convincing proofs I see of this truth, that God governs in the affairs of man and if a sparrow cannot fall to the ground without his notice is it probable that an empire can rise without his aid?"

Benjamin Franklin

"I realize another thing, that in this world fast runners do not always win the race and the brave do not always win the battle, wise men do not always earn a living..." Ecclesiatics9:11

KNOWLEDGE, HUMILITY

Knowledge is the ability to comprehend with the conscious man. It is the ability to posses information, understanding or awareness of something. To be at the top of any endeavor involves knowledge. Talent is not enough without the knowledge to utilize it to the maximum. The science fiction film "The x-men" adapted from the comic series "x-men" is based on a professor (professor Xavier) getting talented youths with uncanny abilities (mutants) to use their trained raw abilities to form a force to protect humanity. He gave them knowledge on how to use their talents. Bill Gates did not invent the computer. He used residual knowledge to develop the graphical interface called windows. The playwright William Shakespeare said that "life is a stage and every body has come to play his part." Every modern day scientific invention is based on the principles discovered by others. No man is an embodiment of knowledge. It is the small part of ignorance that we arrange and classify as knowledge. William Shakespeare himself studied poetry from the Italians whom he copied the pattern of poetry called the sonnet. Some of the scientific discoveries were in different parts of the world. Electric lamp by Thomas Edison (U.S), electric motor (D.C) by Zenobe Grammar (Belgium) microscope by Zechariahs Jansen (Dutch), telephone by J Philips Reis (German), logarithm by John Napier (Scots). Now the above were possible in the European countries because they consciously embarked on an Industrial revolution. The issue here today is that the present complicated computers were built because men borrowed bits of most of the earlier inventions like electricity. Knowledge is like picking a scattered ceramic-ware. It is scattered all over the world. Ola Rotimi the renowned Nigerian playwright used residual knowledge based on the works of Sophocles (Oedipus Rex) of Greece origin to write the play "The gods are not to blame). This complex (Oedipus complex) was also analyzed by Sigmund Freud an Australian psychiatrist. Any knowledge of authority in educational book is based on plagiarism euphemized to research. Plagiarism is total photocopy while research is photocopying from different books. It is lack of knowledge that makes teams have coaches.

1) The wisest man is he who thinks himself the least so.
2) One of the greatest pieces of economic wisdom is to know what you do not know.
3) It is unwise to be sure of one's own wisdom. It is healthy to be reminded that the strongest might weaken and the wisest might err.
4) The age of Methuselah has nothing to do with the wisdom of Solomon.
5) Only one too stupid to find his way home would wear himself out with work. ecclisiatics10: 11

Once, some students were asked in Babylon. "A bag heavy with gold or clay tablet carved with words of wisdom, if you have your choice. Which do you choose."

"The gold, the gold", chorused all the students. "Hark!" the teacher continued "Hear the wild dogs out. There in the night. They howl and wail because they are lean with hunger. Yet feed them and what do they do? Fight and strut. They fight and strut some more, giving no thought of tomorrow that will surely come. Just so it is with the sons of men. Give them a choice of gold and wisdom – what do they do? Ignore the wisdom and waste the gold. On the morrow wait, because they have no more gold."

If a man empties his purse into his head, no man can take it away from him. An investment in knowledge always pays the best interest.

Education is that which discloses to the wise and disguises from the foolish their lack of understanding. He who opens a school door, closes a prison. Our progress as a nation can be no swifter than our progress in education.

There is no use whatever trying to help people who do not help themselves. You cannot push anyone up a ladder unless he be willing to climb himself. People seldom improve when they have no other model but themselves to copy after.

KNOWLEDGE

There are more men enabled by study than by nature. The more we study, the more we discover our ignorance. The wisest mind has something yet to learn.

Wear your learning like watch, in a private pocked, and do not pull it out and strike it merely to show that you have one. One good schoolmaster is worth a thousand priests.

HUMILITY: This is the ability to throw away ego and learn from those who know it better than you do. Jesus Christ simply put this way "Blessed are the meek for they shall inherit the earth". All wish to possess knowledge, but few, comparatively speaking are willing to pay the price.

I was not born to write. I simply craved the art of writing and started writing but that was not enough. I did research on how to write. I was attending classes with junior students where I was working to learn English language properly while I had finished and passed the subject with an A, over ten years ago. I was the laughing stock of every student as I was visibly old in the class. The lecturer a good Ghanaian also called me to find out if I was writing an exam. I told him I was only increasing my knowledge.

It sure did help me. Here I am today writing, a man from pure science and engineering background. You must have knowledge of the relevant area you are tending to life and also be flexible to change as the tide is changing. There are new things every day on career. Are you still using Olympic typewriters when we are at the age of the Internet?

(1) Without humility there can be no humanity.
(2) This is the very best of man to find out about his own imperfections.

The mind of the scholar, if he would leave it large and liberal, should come in contact with other minds.

PERFECTION

This is the ability to be complete or correct in every way conforming to a standard or ideal with no omissions, errors, flaws or extraneous elements. God himself is a perfectionist. We were told from the account of creation in the bible that God saw what he had done and it was good. It pleased him. Have you ever weeded your house and felt satisfaction at the beauty that comes out as a result? Most people in the so-called third world countries crave for goods in Europe. The reason is simply Europe's, knack to do things that are durable. This is possible because any goods made in Europe or imported to Europe have to be standardized before consumers can use it. If your axe is blunt and you don't sharpen it you have to work harder to use it. Ecclesiastics 10:10

(1) Aim at perfection in most things they who aim at it, and persevere will come much nearer to it than those whose laziness and despondency make them give it up as unattainable.
(2) Perfection is attained by slow degrees it requires the hand of time.
(3) Practice makes perfect.
(4) Whatever is worth doing at all is worth doing well.
(5) Be a finisher. Finish what you start.

VIRTUES

Virtue is a quality of great moral value. One of the virtues people of the third world lack is punctuality which is a negative trend which we call "*The African man time*" such attitude give the impression of one who is unserious. Africans will only keep to time when it is time to collect money, see my poem *"pay day."* A little leaven leavens the whole lump, no serious minded man would want to entrust his business to a man that is not time conscious. How is he sure you will not disappoint him latter. He who is faithful in little things will not be faithful in big things. Men in developed countries are very time conscious that is why they have reminders and alarms. Those are not *"toy watches"*. Buy an electronics alarm watch or write your appointment days and time. Another often-neglected virtue is: *trustworthiness*. The fruits of dishonesty are sweet but it is ephemeral. The taste will only last when the sweet is in the mouth. Once you have been branded as a dishonest person, it is difficult to remove that smear. The victim will simply use the principle "Once beaten twice shy" or a local adage that says "A man who was once beaten by a snake will run at sighting an earthworm." The negative effect of dishonesty can be best illustrated in one of Aesop's fables "Crying wolf." The story goes that once upon a time a Shepard boy was fond of crying "wolf is here" and people will rush out with guns, machetes and all manner of instrument to attack the wolf but at the end he will tell them that the wolf has gone. He did it for the second time and no wolf. When he cried wolf the third time that the wolves actually came every body thought he was joking as usual and refused to go to his rescue. This time the wolves ate all their sheep.

"You can fool some of the people all the time, and all of the people some of the time but you cannot fool all the people all the time." Abraham Lincoln

APPEARANCE

(1) Even if a wolf wears a sheep's clothing, he will be ushered in first as a sheep before you will discover he is a wolf. Learn to dress as it suites the occasion and profession, don't be an odd man. Be neat inwardly and outwardly. Cleanliness is next to godliness. You don't have to have plenty of clothes to be neat, if you cannot be neat in the little you have you cannot be neat in the boxes you have. That will even be move strenuous to maintain.

(2) You may turn into an archangel, a fool, or a criminal- no one will see it. But when a button is missing every one sees that.

(3) When I see a bird that walks like a duck and swims like a duck and quacks like a duck, I call that bird a duck.

(4) A man is not like a tortoise that carries its house on its back. Except people who have known you, nobody knows you live in a mansion by your looks, but people can feel you are from the forest by the thorns that stick on your clothes.

(1) If your can be well without health you may be happy without virtues.

(2) Perfect virtues is to do un-witnessed that which we should be capable of doing before the entire world.

(3) The person who talks most of his own virtues is often the least virtuous.

(4) Virtues consists not in abstaining from vice, but not desiring it.

(5) The only reward of virtue is virtue.

PART B

SETBACKS
WHEN THEY COME AND
ARE INEVITABLE

When you are aspiring to the highest places it is honorable to reach the second or even the third rank.

AFFLICTIONS

(1) "The germ cannot be polished without friction. No man is perfected without trials." A Chinese proverb.
(2) Strength is born in the deep silence of long-suffering hearts, not amid joy.
(3) Affliction, like the iron-smith shapes as it smites.
(4) Affliction can bring you much closer to your God and you will be very happy it came because of the knowledge you get in the closeness.
(5) As threshing separates the wheat from the chaff, so does the affliction purify virtues.
(6) Affliction comes to us, not to make us sad but sober, not to make us sorry but wise.

ADVERSITY

(1) Adversities make some people men and prosperity make some people monsters.
(2) Little minds are tamed and subdued by misfortune but great minds rise above them.
(3) Prosperity in not without many fears and distastes adversity not without many comforts and hope.
(4) The good things of prosperity are to be wished, but the good things that belong to adversity are to be admired.
(5) Prosperity is a great teacher adversity is greater. Possession pampers the mind. Privation trains and strengthens it.
(6) Poverty is a teacher if you realize. It can teach the true value of the gifts useful to life.

INJUSTICE

(1) If though suffer injustice, console thyself. The true unhappiness is in doing it.
(2) Those who commit injustice bear the greatest burden.
(3) He who commits injustice is ever made wretched than he who suffers it.
(4) In this world full often our joys are only the tender shadows, which our sorrows cast.
(5) The darkest part of the night is usually before light will start shining. Your light will soon start shining.
(6) "Avenge not yourselves but rather give place unto wrath for it is writhen vengeance is mine, I will repay saith the lord."   Romans 12:19
(7) Revenge is the abject pleasure of an abject mind.

PAIN

(1) Pain dies quickly and lets her weary prisoners go: the fiercest agonies have shortest reign.
(2) Pain and pleasure like light and darkness succeed each other.

(3) Into each life some rain must fall.

(4) There can be no rainbow without a cloud and a storm.

(5) Out of suffering have emerged the strongest souls.

(6) "...but we soon became conditioned like the shell of tortoise under rain and shine as we soon became hardened and we cut into hard steel like knife cuts into butter, for when a man carries an ocean a lake became like a feather for him." (An excerpt from my anthology "Political Irony and other poems.")

(7) The salvation of the world is in men's suffering.

(8) The world is a comedy to those who think, a tragedy to those who feel.

(9) The past if it is bad can be a lesson. Those who cannot remember the bad past are condemned to repeat it. Remember the past and learn, but burn it up like ashes.

(10) Study the past if you will divine the future.

(11) The present contains nothing more than the past, and what is found in the effect was already in the cause.

(12) Death is a call to higher service.

(13) Everyone is a moon and has a dark side, which he never shows to anybody.

(14) When two rocks meet; the rock in affliction and the rock in a man; the harder will make the weaker crumble. Which are you?

(15) An obstacle in front of a stream makes the stream look for other outlets, when one door in closed many more will be opened.

(16) One thing is certain, no matter how dark the night is, light must still come with time. There is a solution to your problem.

(17) A hundred men in front of a moving train will not stop it from getting to its destination, be a moving train.

(18) The face of a he-goat will not put fear on the owner to stop it from entering the pot. No matter how your afflictions look like, they must enter your pot.

(19) *Your not having it yet after all your efforts indicates that: that is not God's time yet or you are not praying persistently or that is not the will of God for you or you are not following proper procedures spiritually or physically.*

(20) When you fall on your face it keep your knees in a position to pray and when you fall on your side it makes one leg to kick and one hand to grasp or punch, and when you fall on your head it makes

your legs to be a weapon and when you fall on your feet it makes your head see clearer and if you fall on your back, your face to look at the sky.

(21) Trees that have deep roots will always grow new branches even if it is felled.

(22) A bag full of liquid will stand upright.

(23) The many holes in a gas canister make more holes for gas escapes.

(24) Cutting only the branch of a tree will not kill it. The downfall of a man is not the end of his life.

(25) A hard ball will give a hard bounce when it falls on a hard floor.

(26) Springs are compressed to make them push hard and arrows stretched to make them shoot farther, your stretch will take you farther.

(27) A ball that is full of air bounces higher when it hits a hard floor. You will bounce higher.

(28) A bird will not stop to be a bird even if it stops flying and starts walking.

(29) When a man falls it is an opportunity for him to see the pants of his limitations from ground.

(30) When a wave comes under your boat it makes it go higher and further. Your afflictions will make you go higher and further.

(31) The darkest time of the night indicates the coming of the morning light. Your afflictions show that your light is near.

(32) A hard ball will always bounce on any side it falls because every part of it is full of air, bounce off that situation.

(33) A fallen elephant will still be a problem to lift to the house of he who set the trap for it. You will be a problem to your enemies.

(34) When a man pulls you down he comes down with you.

(35) Weeping is but for a moment but joy will come soon.

(36) There is no amount of tears that will drown a handkerchief.

(37) Death is a price everybody has to pay.

ATTACKS FROM OTHERS- SKEPTISM, JEALOUSY, SARCASM

(1) The path of sound credence is through the thick forests of skeptism.

(2) Skeptism is the chastity of the intellect.

(3) The worthiest people are the most injured by slander, as the best fruit the fruit the birds have been pecking.

(4) Skeptism brings out the best in you.

(5) To avoid critism do nothing, say nothing be nothing.

(6) It is only important events that are in the news. See yourself as an important event being talked about.

(7) Remember that nobody will ever get ahead of you as long as he is kicking you in the seat of the pant.

(8) Critism makes you check around you. Looking back is not a sign of fear for a lion it is a sign of caution.

(9) A cynic is a man who, when he smells flowers, looks around for a coffin.

(10) The cynic is one who never sees a good quality in a man and never fail to see a bad one.

(11) Analyze good critisms, as there may be some truth in it to your perfection.

(12) Ask the critic what he has done himself.

(13) Let a Wiseman rebuke you and you will become wiser.

(14) It is better to receive the rebuke of a Wiseman than the praises of fools.

ATTITUDE TOWARDS CRITISMS can better be explained by the poetry "Why they say I am crazy"

WHY THEY SAY I AM CRAZY

I refused to dance when on the drums they pound.
But prefer to muse in the hours of the noon.

I refused to muse when they wail and mourn,
but prefer to stand, moon in the noon,

since they were not there when my maker made me here, how can
I a life in whims and caprices of others be? Let me be! For so say they
of David of old, as of joy he danced to himself bold, that insane he was
they swore, just because he refused to be the man they want.

Dread locked Rasta they are, just the same taste they lacked, names insane they called. Then what say they of the locks of old? Whose laws of God they hold, that God a fool he was?

Or beards that sweep the ground, when on robes are crowned, that suits coats and the ties, would laugh to scorn at times, just because they wont be coats and ties,

my thoughts carried to a man, whose house birds that eat worms passed, said he to them "Eat my food the best to see", only for him to call on the birds to live who offered him worms they have to give, the best they have to eat.

Yes, I work in the negative sides, to work the majestic strides. A king crowned by non, but in hearts I rule of all, a castle a man's home is the king of my life I want to be. Not to dance to the drums they pound. Insane a way I sound, to be the must I must be.

Akimua Timitimi

THE MAN WITH MANY LOOKS

Once upon a time, a young man wore a new clothe that his father bought for him and asked his friends how he looked. "You look ridiculous," said his friend who was rather very tall. "You should have been as tall as I am then you could have good fitting," he said.

The young man went to another of his friends who was rather too short. He said "You look too ridiculous in your new clothes if you had been a bit shorter you could have had more fittings".

The young man continued his journey and saw another of his friends who was rather very fat, he said "You are rather too slim", he said "You could have been fat and good fitting".

The young man went to another of his friends and met his friend who was rather too fair in his complexion Had it been you were fair you could have looked better" he told him. So did his dark friend and the one with fat lips and so on told him what he could have looked better with.

The young man now weary from his stroll laid down to sleep and had a dream. In this dream half of his body was fat, half thin, half short, half fair, half dark and half tall. In his new look he walked to his friends who started laughing uncontrollably on seeing him. He went to look at a mirror and saw how ridiculous he was and was frightened. Suddenly he woke up with a jostle and thanked God that it was only a dream. The young man now very happy about his person and his looks as he moved on proudly, resolved to be himself and not others would want him to be.

HOW TO OVERCOME AFFLICTIONS, WORRIES, PAINS ETC.

Transmutation: Transmutation is the art of causing something to change in nature, and substance. In this technique one consciously occupies himself with something else. He redirects his energy to something more creative. I wrote this book and my first novel as a result of transmutation. In my first novel "the price of the buffalos," universities were on strike, how best could I spend my time? I considered playing football, but on second thought I wont get money from it now, so I decided to write to make money. I wrote this book the one you are now reading out of boredom in the office. There are a lot of things to occupy your mind with. Invest in church work, social services, sports clubs and associations. Do chores at home, help others, there is dignity in labour.

(1) "As a cure for worry work is better than Whiskey."
     Ralph Waldo Emerson
(2) Mucus cannot grow on a rolling stone.
(3) The reason why worry kills more people than work in that more people worry than work.

THE POWER OF THE BIBLE: Weather you believe it or not there is potency which I do not understand in reading a verse of the bible every day first thing in the morning especially the psalms, it has spiritual healing effect on the spirit.

SUPERNATURAL: prayer, pray to God to lift that burden off you."
is any afflicted let him pray..." James 5:13

"There is nothing that wastes the body like worry and one who
has any faith in God should be ashamed to worry about anything
whatsoever."

Mahatma Gandhi

YOUR PERSONALITY

This is the total of the psychological, intellectual, emotional and
physical characteristics that make up the individual especially as others
see him. Personality is to a man what perfume is to a flower. The
standard of every personality is the attributes of God. For every human
being has his limitations. Following a man as standard is like swallowing
a fish whole, you will enjoy a bit of its sweetness, and you will also have
taken in the bones, intestines and shit. No man is perfect in all areas.
We only know in part. There no such thing as *'a self made'* man. We
are made up of thousands of others. Everyone who has ever done a kind
deed for or spoken one word of encouragement to us has entered the
make-up of our character and of our thoughts as well as our success.

(1) Personality can be termed as our attitudes and habits.
(2) Personality can be improved.

THINGS THAT MAKE OUR PERSONALITIES, LEADING TO OUR DESTINY

(1) **HABITS:** this is a tendency to repeat an act again and again. It is
     a behavioral pattern that has a degree of automatism.
(2) Habits begin like cobwebs and end up in iron chains.
(3) Each year, one vicious habit rooted out in time out to make the
     worst man good.
(4) The chains of habits are too weak to be felt until they are too strong
     to be broken.

(5) Habits if not resisted, soon become necessity.

(6) Let us not say, every man is the architect of his own fortune, but let us say, every man is the architect of his own character.

(7) Opinions alter but characters are only developed.

(8) People must look at you as well as into you.

(9) Character is not made in crisis it is only exhibited.

(10) To be in good moral condition requires at least as much training as to be in good physical condition.

(11) You will never be the person you can be if pressure, tension and discipline are taken out of your life.

(12) We all are living things animals and humans, one of differences between the animals and humans is that animals can defecate and make love in public but humans are not supposed to do so.

(13) Grass is sweet but the dog said "if it eats grass they will call him a goat so he does not eat it."

A local proverb

(14) What we do on some great accession will probably depend on what we already are, and what we are will be the result of previous years of self-discipline.

(15) Man is still responsible. He must turn the alloy of modern experience into steel of mastery and character. His success lies not with the stars but with himself. He must carry on the fight of self-correction and discipline.

(16) He that has learned to obey will know how to command.

(17) If the self-discipline of the free cannot match the iron discipline of the mailed fist, in economic, scientific and all other kinds of struggles as well as the military, then the peril of freedom will continue to rise.

(18) He who talks much cannot talk well. Silence is foolish If we are wise, but wise if we are foolish, they always talk who never think and who have the least to say.

(19) Justice is the firm and continuous desire to render to every one that which his it is due.

(20) Speaking much is a sign of vanity, for he that is lavish with words is a niggard indeed.

(21) A man's own good breeding is the best security against other people's ill manners.

(22) Manners easily and rapidly mature into morals.

(23) Moderation in temper is always a virtue; but moderation in principle is always a vice.

(24) He will always be a slave who does not know how to live upon a little.

(25) It is easy for somebody to be modest, but it is difficult to be modest, when one is a nobody.

(26) Modesty may make a fool seem a man of sense.

(27) The greatest conqueror is he who overcomes the enemy without a blow or a word.

(28) People do not seem to realize that their opinion of the world is also a confession of character.

(29) A good name, like a good will is got by many actions and lost by one.

(30) A reputation once broken may possibly be repairable, but the world will always keep their eyes on the spot where the crack was.

(31) What people say behind your back is your standing in your community.

(32) Restraint is the better part of might.

(33) Behavior is a mirror in which every one displaces his image.

(34) Degeneracy follows every autocratic system of violence, for violence inevitably attracts moral inferiors. Time has proven that illustrations tyrants are succeeded by scoundrels.

HUMAN RELATIONSHIP

One of the most used ladders in the attainment of goals is humans. No wonder there are adages coined to suit this ladder "**Man is God to man**" "**No man is an island**" etc.

The golden rule can best be expressed in terms of human relationship "As a man sowed so shall he reap". In every action there is an equal and opposite reaction "Be kind to the people you meet on your way up because you may meet them on your way down" these are all bits of the golden rule.

Joseph the dreamer of the Bible fame was able to get his link to Pharaoh because of the help he rendered to the steward earlier who in turn connected him to Pharaoh. Rahab was spared because of the help she gave to the spies.

The widow got a reward from Elisha because of food she offered to Elisha.

God uses man also as a medium to help or bless man. Hostility breeds hostility. Friendliness breeds friendliness this is a universal law of nature. No wonder in the business world public relations officers are expected to be very friendly and smart.

The golden rule **"as you want others to do unto you so do ye also to them".**

1) An inexhaustible good nature is one of the most precious gifts of heaven spreading itself like oil over troubled sea of thought, and keeping the mind smooth and equable in the roughest weather.
2) The only way to have a friend is to be one.
3) If a man does not make new acquaintances as he advances through life, he will soon find himself left alone; one should keep his friendship in constant repair.
4) Friendship is one mind in five bodies.
5) The best way to keep a friend is not to give them away.
6) People are lonely because they build walls instead of bridges.
7) Language has created the word loneliness to express the pain of being alone, and the word solitude to express the glory of being alone.
8) If there is anything better than to be loved it is loving.
9) Love gives itself it is not brought.
10) To murder character is as truly a crime as to murder the body; the tongue of the slanderer is brother to the dagger of the assassin.
11) A man who builds his name on the ruins of another's fame is worthy to be hated.
12) Never throw mud. You may miss your mark but you will have dirty hands.
13) Wear a smile and have friends; wear a scowl and have wrinkles. What do we live for if not to make the world less difficult for each other?
14) There are many kinds of smiles, each having a distinct character. Some announce goodness and sweetness, others betray sarcasm,

bitterness and pride, some often the countenance by their languishing tenderness, others brighten by their spiritual vivacity.

15) The wealth of a soul is measured by how much it can feel, its poverty by how little.

16) To be proud and inaccessible is to be timid and weak.

17) Pride is an admission of weakness; it secretly fears all competitions and dreads all rivals.

18) The infinitely little have a pride infinitely great.

19) Tolerance is the oil which takes the friction out of life.

20) Tolerance comes with age. For the old will see no fault committed that he himself could not have committed at some time as the other.

21) It is our own vanity that makes the vanity of others intolerable to us.

22) To be a man's own fool is bad enough; but the vain man is everybody's.

23) The only cure for vanity is laughter and the only fault that is laughable is vanity.

24) When you try to pull a man you will come down with him.

25) Don't expect to build up the weak by pulling down the strong.

Human relationships can be best seen in these stories;
"The lion and the river"
"Why people don't play with snakes"
"Why people chase mosquitoes away"

THE LION AND THE RIVER

Once upon a time when the lion ruled all the jangle, there was a river that people loved visiting. Although the king was very rich and powerful with beautiful gardens, the animals did not visit him the way they visited the river.

The king was worried about this trend and wanted to find out the secret of the river. So very early in the morning, he went to see the busy river. On sighting the lion the river rose up in a wave and prostrated and said "oh king what has brought you here?". Hurriedly, he sent for his household to bring water and food for the king to drink and eat. After the king had eaten to his full the river called the creatures living with him to sing beautiful songs for him. The frogs sang first with his brothers answering "em emem". After the frog had sang, the river birds sang and flew around colorfully to entertain the king. The king was already carried away by all these friendliness showered on him. Soon the fishes that flew on water and some others in their kinds came and displayed and danced on the way. The lion seeing that he had far spent the night, beckoned to the river that he wanted to have a word with him. He said "how do you make so many people come to you who live at the end of the jungle and people don't come to me who is the king of the jungle?"

In reply the river said "I offer the people a lot of services oh king and they are happy when they are around me that is why they come to me."

The lion on hearing this went back home with his head bent because he did not want to part with anything for his subjects.

WHY PEOPLE DON'T PLAY WITH SNAKES

Once upon a time in the land of animals, the snake which had hands and legs but without teeth lived happily with other animals. However as time went on it soon started developing teeth and became arrogant.

One day the rat was playing with it but it abused and bit it. The rat went home crying. Soon the lizard came to play with it but it fought with it, hissed and abused it. Whoever played with it, he wanted to show off his strength and his new teeth. Soon all the other animals heard about the snake and decided not to play with it again. The snake soon discovered it had no friends again in the animal world and went to play with humans.

Initially it pretended it was good as it was always quite and walked slowly alone, so they started playing with it. In no time it started hissing, abusing them and fighting with them. It bit and injured many of their children. After some time, all the humans held a meeting and decided that they would take it to the king of all the animals and the humans. The king then asked his guard to cut its hands and legs and said that anybody who saw it should throw stones at it. That is why people don't play with snakes and it doesn't have hands and legs and people throw stones at it.

WHY PEOPLE CHASE MOSQUITOES AWAY

Once upon a time. In the land of humans lived the mosquito with humans. The humans used to invite it into their homes, eat with it, and even allow it to sleep and play with their children. Then humans didn't use to beat their children and fight with one another. Although the mosquito was a very small insect it told a lot of stories and lied a lot.

One day when the hunter he was staying with came back from the forest, he told him that his children called him a bushman because he was always going to the bush to hunt. He said so in order to retaliate because they did not give him fruits they had picked.

The man who was short tempered got angry and started beating whoever the mosquito stood on. The mosquito would stand on somebody and say "This one also called you a bushman". "So I am a bush man", the hunter said and gave his first son a slap without waiting for him to explain. He did that to all his children who started crying and feeling pains.

The mosquito who was now enjoying how the children cried also told him that his neighbour who was a fisherman was also calling him a bush man. He went and stood on the fisherman's shoulder and said it was this one that called you a bushman. The hunter who loved to show his strength went straight and slapped the fisherman. The fisherman who was very surprised could not bear it any longer retaliated when the hunter slapped him again. Soon a fight broke out in the town as the fisherman's brothers and the hunters brothers came out.

The king got to hear of it and called everybody to the palace. When they told their stories and the king found out that the mosquito was the cause of the fight. He banished mosquito from the land and put a law that no human should allow the mosquito into their homes. That is why people put nets in their windows and spray the mosquito with insecticides.

Whenever the mosquito comes to whisper to the ears of humans, they chase it away because they do not want to hear lies again.

LADDERS TO A HAPPY MARRIED LIFE

1) **Openness:** A closed safe is suspicion for a would-be robber than the totally opened one.
2) The husband who wants a happy marriage should learn to keep his mouth shut and his checkbook open.
3) A good husband should be deaf and a good wife should be blind.
4) An archeologist is the best husband any woman can have, the older she gets, the more interested he is in her.
5) A woman is not made to be the admiration of all, but the happiness of one.
6) Your spouse as well as being your spouse must also be a tender and intimate friend.
7) Do unto your spouse as you will want your spouse to do unto you.

LADDERS TO LONGIVITY

Just as we have steps as ladders to attain our goals in any endeavor, there are also ladders to attaining longevity. Some of the ladders researchers have made are:-

1) **Good health**: This comes as a result of good health habit such as regular exercise, healthy environment (pollution free environment) stress free living, eating of non-toxic food, intake of essential vitamins and nutritional food.
2) **Genetic factors** have also been linked to longevity. If all factors (act of God) are excluded discoveries have been made that genetic inheritance can also increase longevity.
3) **Divine knowledge**

   (a) Example Moses – His natural force was not abated – working with God – Deuteronomy 34:17
   David mention that by will a man can extend his life. Psalm 90:10

   (b) By setting goals: Goal setting in one's life can make a man want to live. Paul in the Bible had a problem where his goals were almost finished. Life was a monotonous routine so he said he was in a dilemma weather to live or to die but changed his mind by will to live because he has set a goal for himself. Philipians1:21-25

The psalmist expressed goal setting as means of creating will for himself.

"I shall not die, but live and declare the works of the lord". Psalm 118:17.

Clue to getting will: After accomplishing a goal set more targets. There are lots of tasks one can be involved in, lots of research projects for one's self and for others. If all things being equal removing the acts of God, (fires, disasters, wars) one can live long by will.

1) If wrinkles must be written upon our brows, let them not be written upon the breast. The spirit should never grow old.
2) Age is a matter of feeling not of years.
3) Age does not depend upon years, but upon temperament and health. some men are born old, and some never grow old.
4) A man is not old as long as he is seeking something.
5) Don't think of retiring from the world until the world will be sorry that you retire.
6) A man is known by the company that keeps him on after retirement.

Peter in the Bible could not have put it better; he realized that half knowledge was very dangerous. Faith alone is not enough. Diligence alone is not enough. It is a combination of many factors or ladders that can take one to his destiny or his proposed goal.

"...And besides this, giving all diligence, add to your faith virtue, and to virtue knowledge and to knowledge temperance and to temperance patience; and to patience godliness; and to godliness brotherly kindness; and to brotherly kindness charity..." II peter 1:5-7.

About ignorance ..... they that are unlearned and unstable wrest, as they do also the other scriptures, unto their own destruction. 2 peter 3:16.

MAINTAINING YOUR SUCCESS

It is a common story in history that a kingdom very powerful rose, conquered kingdoms and latter another kingdom more powerful rose conquered the previous ones, a vicious circle. Why couldn't kingdoms retain their premiership, retain their dominion, research shows that kingdoms which were once powerful and latter collapsed were due to relaxed principles.

After looting and conquering, the once-disciplined soldiers looked at the women, the spoils of war, the drinks and soon relaxed their guide over the years; other ambitious kings started training and soon over powered the drunken soldiers. They too soon fell if they do not retain their first zeal. Same story goes with musicians overseas after a hit they are bankrupt.

1. Winning is not a thing to be done once, it is a habit to be maintained.
2. To maintain a winning habit, you must know the pros and cons of your proposed pursuit.
3. You must be abreast with modern and new technologies and good knowledge in respect to your pursuits.
4. You must have proficient workers and zealous successors.
5. You must have the same zeal you started with or more to keep a flame ablaze, one must continue to pump the stove with the same energy he started with or more.
6. You must have knowledge of wise use of money (meet experienced hands to instruct you on wise investments)
7. You must form the habit of saving.
8. You must control your expenditures (buy only necessary things and not pleasure things)
9. You should invest on business that will multiply and a business that you will still see your capital even if it fails.
10. Seek experts in a business you want to do.
11. You must guide your treasures from loss (good banking and insurance)
12. Insure a future income for retirement and for your offspring's.
13. Don't involve in a dubious business your are not sure of.
14. Supernatural principles (giving, tithing, reasonable charity) "Throw your bread upon waters you will soon find it".

Continuity can be likened to a farm and a farmer, if a farm is prepared for planting and the crops are not weeded or watered all year round the crops soon become chocked up.

He who adds not to his learning diminishes it. Much of the wisdom of one age, is the folly of the next. All that is human must retrograde if it does not advance. Social advance depends as much upon the process through which it is secured as upon the result itself.